REVISED AND UPDATED

AMAZING JOURNEYS

To the Depths of the Ocean

Rod Theodorou

Heinemann Library
Chicago, Illinois

© 2000, 2006 Heinemann Library
a division of Reed Elsevier Inc.
Chicago, Illinois

Customer Service 888-454-2279
Visit our website at www.heinemannraintree.com

Designed by Victoria Bevan, Michelle Lisseter, and Bridge Creative Services
Illustrations by Stephen Lings and Jane Pickering at Linden Artists
Printed and bound in China by WKT

10 09 08 07 06
10 9 8 7 6 5 4 3 2 1

New edition ISBN: 1 4034 8792 8 (hardback)
                   1 4034 8799 5 (paperback)

The Library of Congress cataloged the first edition as follows:
Theodorou, Rod
   To the depths of the ocean / Rod Theodorou.
      p. cm. -- (Amazing journeys)
   Includes bibliographical references and index.
   ISBN 1-57572-484-7
   1. Oceanography -- Juvenile literature. 2. Ocean -- Juvenile literature. I. Title. II. Series: Theodorou, Rod. Amazing journeys.
GC21.5.T.48 2000
551.46--DC21
   99-37169
   CIP

Acknowledgments
The publishers would like to thank the following for permission to reproduce photographs:
BBC: Jeff Rotman p. **16**; NHPA: Norbert Wu, p. **10**, p. **21**, p. **23**; Oxford Scientific Films: David B Fleetman p. **15**, Doug Allan p. **23**, Gerard Soury p. **18**, Howard Hall p. **11**, p. **13**, p. **19**, Kathie Atkinson p. **11**, Ken Smith Laboratory/Scripps p. **25**, Liz Bomford p. **27**, Norbert Wu p. **17**, p. **21**, Paul Kay p. **23**, Peter Parks p. **13**, p. **20**, Steve Early p. **15**; Science Photo Library: NASA p. **6**, Peter Ryan/Scripps p. **24**. Opposite: Bruce Coleman Collection.

Cover photograph of an octopus reproduced with permission of Alamy Images/Jeff Rotman.

Disclaimer
All the Internet addresses (URLs) given in this book were valid at the time of going to press. However, due to the dynamic nature of the Internet, some addresses may have changed, or sites may have changed or ceased to exist since publication. While the author and publishers regret any inconvenience this may cause readers, no responsibility for any such changes can be accepted by either the author or the publishers.

Contents

Introduction   *6*

Journey Map   *8*

At the Surface   *10*

The Teeming Shallows   *12*

The Continental Shelf   *14*

The Twilight Zone   *16*

Deepwater Giants   *18*

Into the Darkness   *20*

At the Ocean Floor   *22*

The Sulfur Vents   **24**

Conservation and the Future   **26**

Glossary   **28**

Find Out More   **30**

Index   **32**

Some words are shown in bold letters, **like this**. You can find out what these words mean by looking in the Glossary.

Introduction

You are about to go on an amazing journey. You are going to climb inside a **submersible**, which is an advanced mini-submarine. You will be lowered off a ship into the swelling waters of the Pacific Ocean. Millions of animals live beneath the waves, each one specially adapted to survive in this hostile environment.

You will begin your journey among glittering silver **shoals** of fish, which are pursued by fast hunters. Then, you are going to descend into the gloomy depths to view an amazing environment. You will see incredible creatures, huge **predators**, and animals unknown to science until very recently.

With the help of a submersible like this, you are about to explore the depths of the mighty Pacific Ocean.

Viewed from space, Earth looks like a "blue planet."
Over 70 percent of its surface is covered by seawater.
These oceans are the most unexplored places on Earth.
Most are over 13,000 feet (4,000 meters) deep. Only
the first 655 feet (200 meters) of the water is warm and
lit by the Sun. The rest is dark and cold, but not lifeless.

Some parts of the ocean are incredibly deep. The Grand
Canyon is a spectacular land **gorge** that is over
5,200 feet (1,600 meters) deep. Compare this to the
deepest part of the Pacific Ocean, the Marianas Trench,
which is nearly 36,000 feet (11,000 meters) deep! What
type of creatures could survive in these freezing depths?

The submersible's hatch is closing. You are
about to find out.

This shows the world's five oceans.

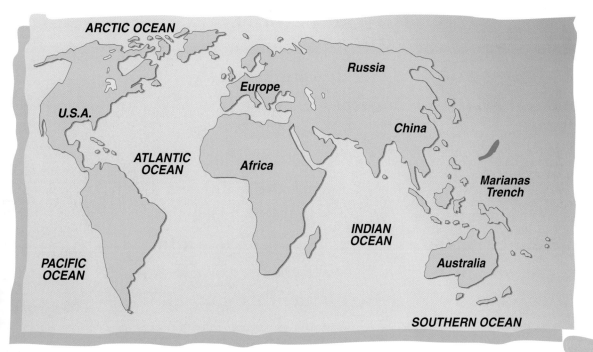

Journey Map

Page 10

Page 12

near shore zone

Page 14

continental shelf

continental slope

Page 16

Here is a map of our underwater journey. You can see that each part of the ocean has a name. We start in shallow waters and move away from the coast, going deeper as we go. This is called the sunlit zone. We will come to the edge of the **continental shelf** and drop down into the deep, open ocean. The sunlight cannot shine deeper than about 650 feet (200 meters). These gloomy waters are called the twilight zone. By the time we reach the 3,300-foot (1,000-meter) mark, it will be completely black outside the **porthole** window. We will need to turn our **submersible**'s lights on to see any life as we sink farther down toward the very bottom of the ocean.

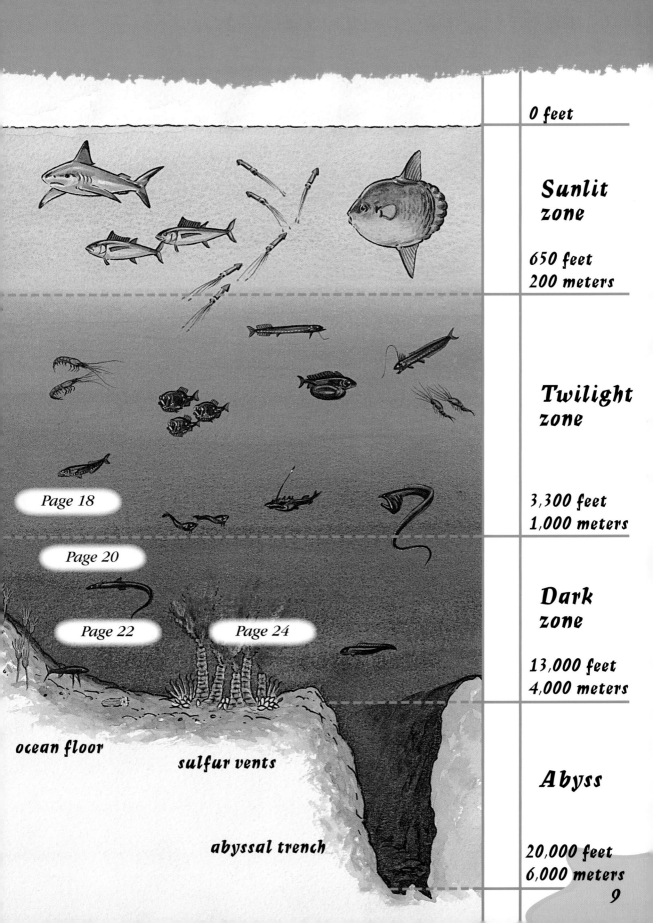

0 feet

Sunlit zone

650 feet
200 meters

Twilight zone

Page 18

3,300 feet
1,000 meters

Page 20

Dark zone

Page 22   Page 24

13,000 feet
4,000 meters

ocean floor

sulfur vents

Abyss

abyssal trench

20,000 feet
6,000 meters

At the Surface

As the **submersible** is lowered over the side of our ship, we have one last look at the sky and waves. Gulls and a **lone** albatross soar overhead. We are lucky enough to see a huge manta ray leap out of the water, frightened by some underwater **predator**. Tiny flying fish also break the surface and glide above the wave crests before disappearing again. With a loud thud, the submersible smacks into the sea. In a burst of bubbles, we sink beneath the surface. The dolphins that have been following our ship soon come to investigate. Bright sunlight glints off the silver fish that pass by in large **shoals**. There is life all around us.

The "wings" of a huge manta ray break the surface of the water.

Portuguese man-of-war

This is actually a **colony** of smaller animals that live together. One acts as a large, gas-filled float that sticks up above the surface and functions as a sail. Others act as stinging **tentacles** that catch food.

Sailfish

This fast hunter has a streamlined body built for speed. It can swim at an amazing 68 miles (109 kilometers) per hour— faster than a cheetah can run!

Flying fish

When the flying fish is chased by a predator, it gathers speed and then jumps out of the water. It spreads out its large fins, which act like wings, carrying the flying fish through the air for about 30 seconds.

The Teeming Shallows

Many of the fish we see in the sunlit zone are dark green-blue on the top and silver underneath. This makes it hard for them to be seen by **predators** from above (looking downward at the green-blue ocean) or below (looking up at the silvery surface).

Invisible to our eyes are millions of tiny **plankton**. The plant-plankton grow in the warm sunlight, while the animal-plankton feed on them and on other tiny food **particles** that are blown toward the ocean's surface by storms or undersea **currents**. Smaller fish feast on this plankton. Larger fish eat the smaller fish. Even giant whales eat the plankton, as well as other tiny shrimps called krill. Without the plankton, most other ocean life would die.

1	ocean sunfish
2	skipjack tuna
3	manta ray
4	Pacific sardine
5	common dolphin
6	blue shark
7	cod
8	dolphin fish
9	krill
10	Pacific right whale
11	basking shark

The shallow water is lit up by the Sun's rays and is full of life.

Plankton

Plankton are microscopic creatures. Some are tiny plants. Others are tiny animals that eat this plant-plankton. Some are fish **fry** or the tiny **larvae** of other sea animals.

Whale shark

At 60 feet (18 meters) long, this is the largest fish in the world. It is completely harmless and wanders the ocean alone, feeding on plankton.

Pacific salmon

Salmon are born in freshwater streams and then **migrate** to the sea. They live in the ocean for several years before traveling huge distances back to the streams where they were born. There, they **spawn** and then die.

The Continental Shelf

The **submersible** dives deeper. We cannot see the ocean surface anymore, but the temperature **gauge** indicates the water is still warm (59 °F, or 15 °C) and there is still a lot of light. We catch sight of the seabed below us. We are now at the **continental shelf**.

The submersible's whining **propeller** blades slow down for a while as we stop to enjoy the life around us. A green turtle flaps slowly by on its way to feed on turtle grass, a kind of seaweed. In front of us, we can see the end of the continental shelf. Soon we will have to go over that cliff edge and descend down the steep continental slope into deeper, darker waters.

1   coral
2   sponges
3   seaweed
4   green turtle
5   barracuda
6   jellyfish
7   hammerhead shark
8   red snapper
9   California sea lion
10   spotted eagle ray
11   Pacific octopus
12   puffer fish
13   moray eel

The continental shelf marks the end of the shallows and the beginning of deeper water.

Blue spotted ray

Like most rays, this one spends much of its life on the seabed, making it hard for **predators** to spot. If attacked, it can also defend itself with the two **venomous spines** in its tail.

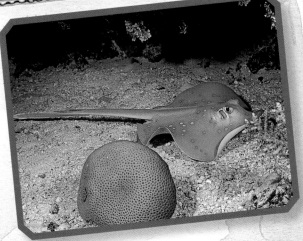

Pacific lobster

This brightly colored **scavenger** hides among rocks during the day. At night, it comes out to feed on worms and other small animals.

Pacific octopus

This giant octopus can grow much bigger than a man! It can have up to a 30-foot (9-meter) arm span, but is a very shy and gentle animal. Its favorite foods are crabs and lobsters.

The Twilight Zone

As we dive deeper down the continental slope, things start to change. It gets much colder. Our temperature **gauge** drops to 41 °F (5 °C). We are so deep we can hardly see any sunlight, so we switch on the **submersible**'s lights.

There are far fewer fish down here, but our lights soon attract them. The deeper we go, the stranger the fish look. Many fish and shrimp here have what look like tiny headlights. They have special **organs** on their skin that produce light. These are used to identify and attract a **mate** or to attract **prey**. Some can "turn on" these lights in a sudden flash of brightness to confuse a **predator**.

These squid have large eyes and light organs to help them see and be seen.

Hatchetfish

Most hunters in the twilight zone look upward to see if they can spot the dark shadow of another fish against the dim light from above. Hatchetfish have light organs along their belly and tail that make them glow just enough to match the light above them. Viewed from below, the fish are almost invisible to predators. Like many fish in the twilight zone, they swim upward at night to feed in the richer, shallower waters when many predators are asleep.

Viper fish

Like many twilight hunters, these fish have huge jaws filled with large fangs and a special fin with a light on the end. This **lure** acts like a fishing pole, attracting smaller prey, which the viper fish gobbles up.

Deepwater Giants

We have been traveling down for over two hours now. Below 650 feet (200 meters), there is so little light that no seaweed or plant life can grow. There is therefore no **plankton** down here. The fish feed on animal **carcasses** or droppings that fall down from above, or they feed on each other.

Suddenly, we pick up something huge on our **radar**. It is two sperm whales, diving straight down into the depths to feed. We peer out of the **porthole**. These incredible whales are shaped like submarines and can dive to amazing depths to hunt for their favorite **prey**, giant squid.

Sperm whales have tiny eyes, but they can find their prey in the darkness using **sonar**.

18

Whipnose angler

The whipnose angler uses its incredibly long **lure** to attract prey nearer and nearer to its hungry mouth.

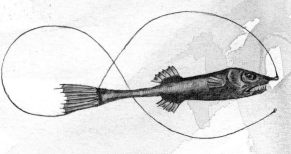

Sperm whale

The huge, blunt **snout** of the sperm whale acts like a heavy weight, helping it sink down quickly into the depths to hunt. The whale can hold its breath for over an hour!

Giant squid

These massive but mysterious animals can weigh over a ton and reach lengths of over 52 feet (16 meters)! Dead bodies of these huge creatures have been washed onto beaches, but they have never been filmed alive.

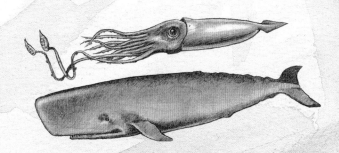

Into the Darkness

We are very deep now—deeper than 3,300 feet (1,000 meters). The incredible weight of the water above us presses down on the **titanium hull** of our **submersible**. This **pressure** would crush a diver like a paper cup. The water is nearly freezing, and there is no light. When we switch off the submersible's lights and look through the thick **Plexiglas porthole**, all we see is inky blackness. Down in this world, many of the animals are completely blind. They are often black, making them hard to see even with our lights back on. There is very little food down here. Hunters will attack and try to gobble up any fish they find, no matter what the size.

Many deep-sea fish, like this dragonfish, have a long thread called a lure that they use like a fishing pole to attract their **prey**.

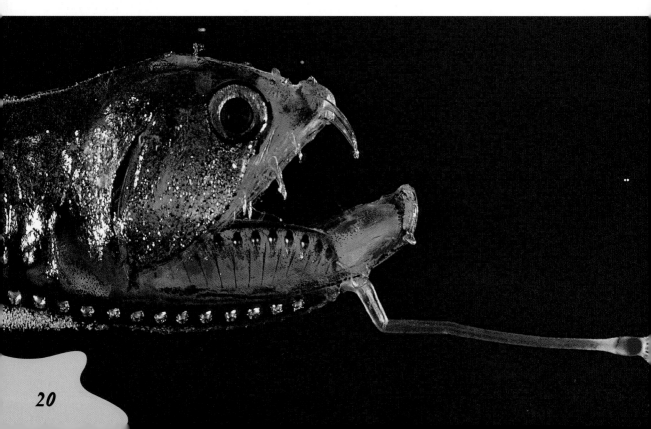

Fangtooth

The fangtooth's mouth bristles with huge teeth. It is also called an ogrefish—for obvious reasons!

Gulper eel

The gulper eel is like a giant swimming mouth. It drifts along until it meets another fish, then it opens its huge mouth and strikes.

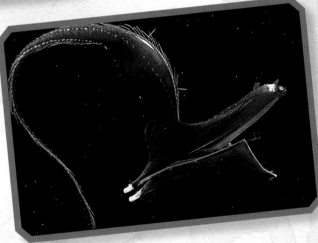

Deep-sea angler

The female anglerfish grows up to 3.3 feet (1 meter) long, but the male is tiny. The male spends its life holding onto the female. She has a **lure** tipped with a light **organ** and a huge bag-like stomach that allows her to eat fish up to twice her own size!

At the Ocean Floor

We are nearly 10,000 feet (3,000 meters) down now. The **hull** of the **submersible** creaks and groans under the enormous **pressure** above. The water outside is below freezing. Suddenly, our lights pick up the ocean floor below.

The surface of the ocean floor is made up of the tiny skeletons and droppings of millions of animals. It forms a thick layer of mud that will stir up into a cloud if touched. There are no corals or clumps of seaweed. There are few signs of life here. It is like a desert. As we move along above the mud, we start to see more and more snails and worms making their way slowly and carefully along the muddy ooze.

1   deep-sea shrimp
2   sea cucumber
3   nudibranch
4   sea urchin
5   sea lilies
6   ratfish
7   halosaur
8   tripod fish
9   brittle star

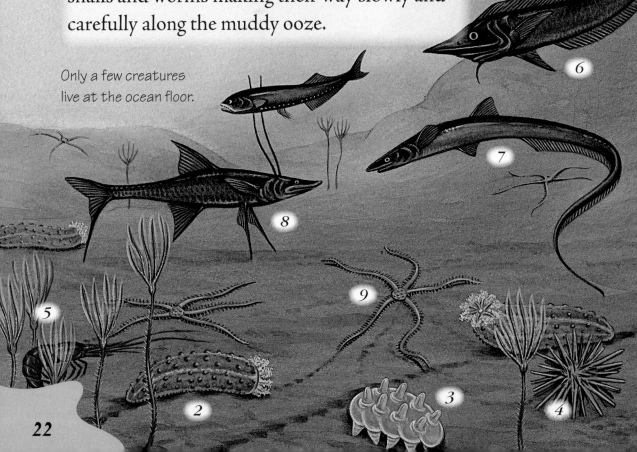

Only a few creatures live at the ocean floor.

Tripod fish

The special fins of this fish help it to "stand" above the ocean floor and wait to catch the **scent** of any food nearby.

Sea spider

This strange, blind creature is not a real spider. It walks along the muddy seabed on its long spindly legs, looking for worms to eat with its tube-like mouth.

Brittle star

These delicate starfish feed on tiny food **particles** they find on the seabed. If an attacker bites off one of their arms, they can grow a new one.

The Sulfur Vents

Suddenly, our temperature **gauge** starts to show warmer water. How could this be? We start to notice more fish. Then, we discover the reason. Deep below us, water is being heated by hot **lava** and shooting up through cracks in the ocean floor. The water carries **minerals** through these cracks, which form large **vents** on the seabed like chimneys. The water is also full of **sulfur**, which is eaten by bacteria. A whole **colony** of amazing animals lives around these chimneys, feeding on this bacteria.

Beyond us is another cliff edge, leading to a deep-water trench. Even we cannot go any deeper. It is time to return to the surface. Who knows what creatures remain to be discovered in this amazing and wonderful world?

Huge worms and clams feed on the sulfur bacteria. Fish, crabs, shrimp, and thousands of anemones also live around the vents.

Tube worms

Huge red worms in long white tubes live around the chimneys. They grow up to 3.3 feet (1 meter) long.

A special world

Until these vents were discovered, it was thought that all life on the planet needed the Sun to survive. Plants cannot grow without sunlight. Without plants, every other life form would die. The amazing thing about the sulfur vents is the animals here do not need sunlight to keep them alive.

Giant clams

Giant 12-inch (30-cm) long white clams also live around the vents.

Conservation and the Future

Pollution

For years, people have treated the oceans like a huge sewer. It was thought that the seas were so big and so deep you could throw anything you wanted into them and it would be washed away. Sewage, garbage, and industrial waste such as petroleum and insecticides were pumped or dumped straight into the sea. Recently, scientists have realized that pollutants do enormous damage in the sea. Many chemicals get eaten by tiny sea creatures, which are then eaten by fish— and finally by people!

Now, many countries have laws to control and stop ocean pollution, but a huge amount of sea dumping still occurs.

Captains of oil tankers still dump huge amounts of unwanted oil into the sea, killing thousands of seabirds.

Overfishing

Many of the fish and whales in the sea have been hunted by humans almost to **extinction**. Modern fishing boats have **sonar** to find the fish and huge nets to catch whole **shoals**. Many larger animals, such as dolphins and sharks, are also caught and killed in these nets by accident. Many countries are trying to control this overfishing. Most whale-hunting has now been banned, but it may be too late for some species of whale, such as the beluga.

One new idea is to create **marine**-protected areas where no one can pollute or kill the wildlife. These nature reserves are one of many ways we can preserve marine wildlife for the future.

The most famous marine-protected area is the Great Barrier Reef Marine Park in Australia.

Glossary

carcass	dead body (usually of an animal)
colony	group of similar things living together
continental shelf	shallow area of seabed between the land and the depths of the water
current	movement of water, sometimes caused by the tide
extinction	when a type of animal or plant dies out and will never live again
fry	young fish
gauge	instrument for measuring or testing something
gorge	very deep, steep valley cut into the ground by a river
hull	frame of a boat or ship
larva	(more than one are called larvae) insect just after it is born
lava	hot, melting rock that comes out of cracks in Earth
lone	only, or on its own
lure	something that lights up on a fish's head so it can attract prey
marine	to do with the sea
mate	when a male and a female come together to have babies
migrate	to move from one place to another, often to feed or mate
mineral	natural substance, usually one that comes from the ground, such as salt
organ	part of a body that does a job to make the body work
particle	very small piece of something
plankton	tiny animal and plant life that floats or swims in water

Plexiglas	very strong, see-through plastic
porthole	window in the side of a ship
predator	animal that hunts, kills, and eats other animals
pressure	weight of something pressing or being pressed
prey	animal that is eaten by predators
propeller	blade that turns quickly to help a vehicle move forward
radar	way of finding things using radio waves
scavenger	something that looks for and feeds on leftovers
scent	smell
shoal	large group of the same type of fish
snout	animal's nose
sonar	(SOund and NAvigation Ranging) way of finding objects, especially underwater, using sound waves
spawn	when water animals lay many eggs together
spine	special stiff or pointed fish fin
submersible	underwater craft used for deep-sea research
sulfur	chemical element
tentacle	long and flexible part of some animals that is used to feel and touch
titanium	silver-gray, light but strong metal
venomous	poisonous
vent	opening for gas or liquid to escape from

Find Out More

Further reading

Baldwin, Carol. *Sharks*. Chicago: Heinemann Library, 2003.

Day, Trevor. *Oceans and Beaches*. Chicago: Raintree, 2003.

Lynch, Emma. *Ocean Food Chains*. Chicago: Heinemann Library, 2005.

Oliver, Clare. *Sea Creatures*. Chicago: Raintree, 2002.

Organizations

Marine Conservation Biology Institute
2122 112th Avenue NE
Suite B-300
Bellevue, Wash. 98004
www.mcbi.org

The Ocean Conservancy
2029 K Street, NW
Washington, D.C. 20006
www.oceanconservancy.org

Using the Internet

If you want to find out more about oceans, you can go to one of the website addresses below. Otherwise, you can use a search engine, such as www.yahooligans.com or www.internet4kids.com, and type in a keyword such as "ocean" or a related subject such as "submersibles."

Websites

www.sanctuaries.noaa.gov

The government's official National Oceanic and Atmospheric Administration (NOAA) web site features a clickable map and profiles of many protected ocean areas.

www.kidsnet.org/seaweb

Follow the links to find out about ocean life, threats to the ocean, and how you can help to protect our seas.

Index

abyss 9

anglerfish 21

clams 24, 25

conservation 27

continental shelf 8, 14

continental slope 8, 14

dark zone 9, 20

dragonfish 20

eels 14, 21

flying fish 11

Great Barrier Reef Marine
    Park 27

hatchetfish 17

krill 12

lobsters 15

Marianas Trench 7

near shore zone 8, 10

ocean floor 9, 22, 24

ocean trenches 7, 9, 24

octopus 14, 15

overfishing 27

Pacific Ocean 6, 7

plankton 12, 13

pollution 26

Portuguese man-of-war 11

predators 10, 11, 15, 16, 17, 19,
    20, 21

rays 10, 12, 14, 15

sailfish 11

salmon 13

sea spider 23

sharks 12, 13, 14, 27

squid 16, 18, 19, 21

starfish 22, 23

sulfur vents 9, 24, 25

sunlit zone 8, 9, 12

tripod fish 22, 23

tube worms 24, 25

twilight zone 8, 9, 16, 17

viper fish 17

whales 12, 18, 19, 27

whipnose angler 19